Retirement:
What Could Go Wrong?
(A Financial Advisor's Perspective)

ROBERT A. NEFF

Copyright © 2019 Robert A. Neff

DISCLAIMER: The material presented in this book is for informational purposes. While care has been taken to present the concepts in an accurate and updated fashion, the author makes no expressed or implied warranty of any kind and assumes no responsibility for errors or omissions. No liability is assumed for incidental or consequential damages in connection with or arising out of the use of the information contained here. The information in this book is intended to provide general information and does not constitute legal, financial, or tax advice.

All rights reserved.

ISBN: 9781713282969

CONTENTS

INTRODUCTION	1
LESSON #1: CAN YOU STOMACH THIS	3
LESSON #2: A "STEP-UP" FROM "ORDINARY"	6
LESSON #3: A FOOL AND HIS MONEY ARE SOON PARTED	9
LESSON #4: ANNUITY ARBITRAGE	11
LESSON #5: WHERE DID MY RETIREMENT PLAN GO?	16
LESSON #6: THE POOR SURVIVOR	19
LESSON #7: INVEST ME NOT	22
LESSON #8: WORK UNTIL WE DIE	25
LESSON #9: COUNTDOWN TO SPEND-DOWN	28
LESSON #10: OH, MY TAX	31
LESSON #11: FREE LABOR	34
LESSON #12: FINANCIAL CONUNDRUM	37
CONCLUSION	41
NOTES	43
ACKNOWLEDGEMENTS	45

ROBERT A. NEFF

DEDICATION

I dedicate this book to my Dad,
Who had such a big heart that God gave him two.
Miss you every day.

Robert D. Neff
1952-2019

INTRODUCTION

I believe that people who have worked, saved and sacrificed over many years deserve to have a successful retirement. The reason for writing this book, and my *WHY,* is that I have witnessed, firsthand, results of decisions people have made which have either significantly increased or significantly decreased their quality of retirement. My goal and hope are that the lessons within can help educate and serve as talking points between retirees and their financial professional and ultimately help avoid some of the not-so-common pitfalls in retirement planning. Remember that *knowledge* is realizing that the street is one way, but *wisdom* is looking both directions anyway.

So, retirement… what could go wrong?

RETIREMENT: WHAT COULD GO WRONG?

LESSON #1

CAN YOU STOMACH THIS

THE STORY

During one of my first interactions with Dean he mentioned that he had a past bad experience with investing in the stock market. When I asked what had happened, Dean told me the following story: Dean had worked at a local Fortune 500 company for several decades and around 2006-2007 had retired due to the increasing health concerns of his wife. In addition, Dean felt he had accumulated a comfortably sized nest egg. The first few years of retirement had been great and he had easily lived off the growth of his nest egg, which was worth close to $750,000. He had been working with an advisor who had suggested an aggressive allocation (a portfolio which attempts to maximize returns by taking on a higher amount of risk). The nest egg had been receiving great returns so he agreed to continue with his advisor's recommendations.

All of this changed, however, as the financial crisis of 2007-2008 began and the stock markets (as well as his investments) began to tumble. What started out at around $750,000 dropped to $300,000. Dean ordered everything to be liquidated. What had started out as a comfortable annual income of approximately $50,000 (including Social Security) would now be fully depleted within the next three to five years, leaving him with only his Social Security benefit to live on. While there may be ways to help prolong his remaining assets, his appetite for the market or anything not guaranteed, was long gone.

THE ISSUES

- Investments not aligned with risk tolerance
- Insufficient funds in cash and conservative accounts to weather a market decline
- Not having enough guaranteed income to cover living expenses
- Longevity risk

THE LESSONS LEARNED

There are several lessons to learn from this particular situation. First, the returns of an aggressively allocated portfolio can be alluring, especially in a long running bull market (things are going great), or a time of economic prosperity. It helps to think of this like walking out on a diving board: the closer one gets to the end of the board, the higher the returns have a potential of reaching (the upswing). However, the downside can be just as far, if not farther (into the water). When building a retirement income plan, it is crucial to make sure a portfolio is built with the client's risk tolerance factored into the plan. If there is one thing that is certain, it is that the market will go up and down. The ride down is when one's ability to handle loss is truly tested.

The second issue is there was not enough cash or other liquid assets set-aside to cover the short-term income needs of the couple. Additionally, having a portion of funds conservatively invested to cover a slightly longer period would certainly help to provide a source of income during market declines. One way to mitigate this kind of situation is to have an income plan based on the "bucket" approach. In this approach, the assets are divided into different time frames and amounts. These assets are then placed into investments with corresponding levels of risk. Typically, funds are distributed into three "buckets" but plans can vary based on risk tolerance, income sources, goals, etc.

1. Cash - meet income needs over short-term
2. Conservative – preservation over returns (typically less than three years)
3. Growth - with a goal of keeping up or outpacing inflation

What is unique about the "bucket" approach is it can give the confidence to stay the course and provide peace during a financial storm. This is one of the reasons it is important to consider working with an experienced retirement income planner to build a unique plan for each couple and their situation.

Lastly by not having a sufficient amount of guaranteed income to cover their cost of living, withdrawals still had to be from the account while the account value was falling. During times of a falling market, each withdrawal from a portfolio further exacerbates the decline of the account and reduces the gain when the fund rises. Guaranteed income can come in many different forms such as Social Security, pensions or annuities and can ultimately help gain control over one of the biggest risks faced in retirement: longevity risk.

Longevity risk happens when people live longer than anticipated life expectancies. As one continues to age, more time is given to experience market volatility, interest rate fluctuation, nursing home cost, legislation changes, etc. which can put a retirement portfolio through all sorts of stresses.

LESSON #2

A "STEP-UP" FROM "ORDINARY"

THE STORY

The next lesson involves a couple, Fred and Paula, who had purchased stock inside of an Individual Retirement Account (IRA) and planned on using the dividends for income in retirement. It was also a primary concern of the couple to leave an inheritance to their two children, who are both high-income earners and in equally high tax brackets. The IRA can be great for tax-deferral purposes. However, as Fred and Paula have almost all of their funds in qualified accounts, the inheritance to their children from these accounts would be taxed at ordinary income rates.

THE ISSUES

- Long-term capital gains rates vs. ordinary income rates
- Required minimum distributions
- Step-up cost basis is valuable for legacy building

THE LESSONS LEARNED

As I have learned over the years, an important part of retirement income planning is to pay attention to the tax efficiency of different types of assets (stocks, mutual funds, bonds, etc.) as well as types of accounts (Retail, Roth, Traditional IRA, etc.). The ability to maximize the tax efficiency of certain assets and to take advantage of current tax laws can lead to a significant impact on taxation, legacy and income. When building a retirement income plan, it is imperative to begin with the end in mind. There are a few other caveats that are worth addressing. I will focus on three that apply to this lesson: ordinary income vs. long-term capital gains rates, RMD's (or Required Minimum Distributions) and the Step-Up cost basis.

First, the primary goal of Fred and Paula was to receive income through dividends. This is great, except one must know that dividends are treated differently depending on whether they are held inside or outside of a retirement account. For example, dividends outside of a retirement account are generally taxed at long-term capital gains rates (if held for one year or more). Long-term capital gains rates are typically lower than ordinary income tax rates and can even be as low as 0%. Dividends inside of a retirement account (excluding Roth IRA's which are tax exempt after some criteria are met) do not receive the same tax benefit and instead are tax deferred. Distributions from the retirement account, including dividends, will then be taxed at ordinary income rates.

Second, let's consider if one has stocks in a tax qualified account such as a Traditional IRA where RMDs would apply. At the time of this writing when one reaches the age of 70½ the government requires account holders to take a distribution from retirement accounts based on life expectancy (or pay a penalty tax of 50% on the amount that should have been distributed). It should be noted however to consult with a tax or financial professional for current RMD requirements because at the time of writing this book there is legislation pending that could change the RMD age from 70.5 to 72. This can be very counter-productive when trying to grow the account to leave a legacy. The government is requiring taxable distributions be made regardless if one is currently in need of the funds or not. Furthermore, this taxable distribution may cause taxable income to increase to a point that Social Security may become taxable or the capital gains tax rate could increase.

The third caveat is called the step-up cost basis. A step-up in cost basis reflects the updated value of an inherited asset. For example, an investor purchased shares at $2 then passes away and leaves the shares (via a beneficiary on the account) to an heir when the shares are $15 means the shares receive a step-up in basis, making the new cost basis for the shares the current market price of $15 [1].

Any capital gains tax paid in the future will be based on the $15 cost basis, not on the original purchase price of $2 [1]. Looking back at Fred and Paula's initial goals of leaving an inheritance for their children, this could be an extremely valuable benefit. Instead of passing on an inheritance that was fully taxable at ordinary tax income rates, as would be the case in a Traditional IRA, a brokerage account could allow the heirs to receive funds at stepped-up cost basis and sell immediately if desired, and pay little to no taxes. *(Remember, tax laws change so make sure to consult with a tax professional.)*

LESSON #3

A FOOL AND HIS MONEY ARE SOON PARTED

THE STORY

A few years back, after Harley passed away and his estate was liquidated, Harley's sole heir received an inheritance. Harley was a divorced man and had suffered numerous health issues for several years prior to his death. Not only was Harley single when he died, he and his sole heir had experienced a rocky relationship and they had been estranged at the time of Harley's death. While death is inevitable and a common part of life, the issue comes about when a beneficiary has only recently become a legal adult, but still lacks the maturity to handle money. In this situation, unfortunately, nearly a quarter-million dollars was squandered on "toys".

THE ISSUES

Having a legally executed Last Will and Testament may get property and other assets to the right place or person, but maybe not at the right time. Estate planning is a key part of any retirement plan.

- Having just a basic Last Will and Testament may not be sufficient planning

- An inheritance for those who can't handle money can do more harm than good

THE LESSONS LEARNED

While a Last Will and Testament makes it easy to name children or heirs as beneficiaries, one issue that needs to be seriously considered is the beneficiary's ability to wisely manage an inheritance. I remember hearing a lesson from Jim Rohn (an American entrepreneur, author and motivational speaker) that really resonated with me, and that message was "How can someone become the ruler of many if they are unable to manage a few?" The same principle applies in this situation. A person will only ever acquire and maintain wealth to the point they are able to manage it.

When individuals who have shown prior lack of wise fund management receive an inheritance, even more devastating results can occur. It's one thing for small problems to compound, but add a few more zeros and things can escalate quickly. For example, lottery winners who have a large sum of money can buy liabilities (things that cost money each year) such as boats, new vehicles, multiple homes, etc. When money runs out, they are still stuck with paying property taxes, maintenance, etc. and cash flow issues really begin (i.e. more out than in).

In cases where the estate beneficiary is young and lacks knowledge or experience in wise fund management, it is imperative to have at least a basic estate plan in effect. The value of having an attorney as well as a financial professional involved, prior to Harley's death, could have had a profound change in outcome. Having a Last Will and Testament can certainly help carry out a person's wishes regarding the distribution of assets and care for minor children. However, to define how, when and what criteria need to be met for funds to be distributed, a testamentary trust or another type of trust may be necessary. My experience has been when instructions for fund distribution are made clear (such as over a specified period or after certain life events happen) the outcome and impact on the heir are generally more positive.

LESSON #4

ANNUITY ARBITRAGE

THE STORY

This next story involves a person that I met at a local event; let's call her Lynn. What initially started as a question about RMD's turned into a significant opportunity to help reduce the tax burden for Lynn's heirs. After a long tenure of teaching and going through a tough divorce, Lynn focused on being frugal with her money. She had learned several different ways to save and invest. Financially, she had done an exceptional job saving and accumulating wealth and now had close to $1 million in investments. Being debt free, a fully paid off home, sufficient income for living expenses and long-term care in place, things looked great. After a discussion about her long-term goals, it was clear she wanted to leave an inheritance for her two children and her grandchildren. One concern she had was both of her children had done exceptionally well in their careers, but were also paying a significant amount in taxes. Lynn preferred the government not be a big benefactor of any gifting plan.

Initially, Lynn planned on just naming her heirs as beneficiaries of a non-qualified annuity (meaning funded with after-tax money) that had been growing for a few years. In fact, what started out as $470,000 in contributions was now worth $550,000. For this lesson, we will just focus on this non-qualified annuity and a possible concept that can address multiple issues.

THE ISSUES

Accumulation of assets is completely different than income and estate planning.

- Tax efficiency and financial leverage
- Tax difference between life insurance and non-qualified annuities
- Tax differences within a non-qualified annuity
- Annuity arbitrage may help maximize benefits for heirs

THE LESSONS LEARNED

After numerous interactions with retirees who desire to leave an inheritance, I hear almost universally (after conversations between parents and their children) that there is "no need for life insurance." However, Tom Hegna (economist, author, and retirement expert) suggests that people spend everything and leave life insurance to the heirs. The reason for this statement is that life insurance proceeds benefits are tax-free, can avoid probate and have the benefit of leveraging the dollar i.e. pennies of premium can equal dollars of benefit.

Look, most heirs do not blatantly say, "Yes, leave me a big inheritance." If they did say that, that should probably disqualify them! The issue we are addressing is tax efficiency and financial leverage. To help make this point, let's start by answering the question, "who sets the minimum price for life insurance?"

Insurance companies set the *minimum* amount or price they will accept to provide a specified death benefit. But who sets the *maximum*? The Internal Revenue Service (IRS). In fact, the IRS realized how efficient life insurance was at minimizing taxes for wealth transfer, so they placed maximum limits on funding of policies while still maintaining the unique tax benefits of life insurance. Now, how does life insurance differ from annuities? Life insurance is to protect against not living long enough and annuities are bought in the event one lives longer than expected. As people live longer, fewer death benefits are paid on life insurance and the life insurance premiums are then used by the insurance company to pay the annuity benefits and vice versa. To begin to see some of the taxation differences, let's now look at non-qualified annuities.

The first major difference between life insurance and non-qualified annuities comes with how benefits from each are taxed. With life insurance, benefits are generally tax-free when received by the beneficiary. Non-qualified annuities, on the other hand, are generally tax-free up to the cost-basis (amount initially invested) and then fully taxable up to the account value. In the case described at the beginning of this lesson, upon the death of Lynn, both of the heirs would receive an equal portion of the non-qualified annuity account value, in this case $275,000, which includes a taxable gain of $40,000 each. The $40,000 each ($80,000 total) is the difference between the original cost basis and the ending account value. Assuming a lump-sum distribution, both beneficiaries would receive a 1099 for their portion of the taxable gain (i.e. $40,000 of taxable gain each).

We can further dissect the taxing of non-qualified annuity in the way that income can be taxed. To better understand this, it is important to know that annuities can be used in one of two phases: distribution or accumulation. An example of an annuity in the distribution phase is when a person is receiving money from a company pension. Generally, all income from a company pension is considered a "gain" because the company contributed the funds to the plan. In a non-qualified annuity, during the distribution phase, however, a portion of the funds distributed is considered a return of premium paid into the annuity until the cost basis is depleted (all of the initial contributions are paid out). As a result, part of the income is excluded from taxation, which is known as the "Exclusion Ratio". During the accumulation phase, distributions made from the annuity (when the annuity has yet to be annuitized and is potentially growing) are generally fully taxable until all taxable gain is distributed and only the initial investment amount (or cost basis) remains. This applies whether distributions are made through a partial surrender or via an income rider. This may be easier to think of as "Last-In, First-Out" (LIFO). Meaning the interest or growth is the last to go into the contract and upon any distribution is also the first to come out.

The last part of this lesson can help address some of the pitfalls mentioned above and bring both life insurance and non-qualified annuities together. This concept is called annuity arbitrage. Annuity arbitrage is when a single premium immediate annuity (payments beginning in less than one year) *and* a life insurance policy

RETIREMENT: WHAT COULD GO WRONG?

is bought to maximize the benefits of each contract. This concept can leverage available assets to increase the inheritance to heirs, surviving spouse, etc. Below is an example of how this could look and some of the benefits that could be realized.'

1. By annuitizing a similarly sized non-qualified annuity:

    a. $550,000 could produce around $33,600/year (to pay the life insurance premium) for individual's entire lifetime with a minimum period of 20 years of benefits given similar current age and interest rates.

    b. Individual's beneficiaries could receive the remainder of the income during that 20-year period, should a premature death occur.

    c. A large majority of the income received could be excluded from taxation due to the "Exclusion Ratio" i.e. a return of premium.

2. Individual could opt to purchase a life insurance policy

    a. Income provided above could fund a ($1,000,000 permanent life policy)

    b. The life insurance proceeds would be tax-free to beneficiaries, upon individual's death.

    c. Proceeds would not go through probate.

What is beautiful about this is that, if structured correctly, the annuity will pay for the life insurance indefinitely so funding will never be an issue. Should individual have a change of mind down the road and want to leave less inheritance or need more income for living expenses, depending on the type of life insurance contract purchased, the face amount or death benefit of the policy may be able to be reduced. A reduction in face amount would reduce the premium accordingly and she could then have more disposable income each year.

Alternatively, if individual passed away sooner than expected, the heirs would receive the remaining annuity payments for the 20-year period (which will be taxed more favorably due to the "Exclusion Ratio"). In addition, the life insurance benefit would pay out tax-free.

LESSON #5

WHERE DID MY RETIREMENT PLAN GO?

THE STORY

This lesson is based on something that happens more often than most would like to admit. It is called the "unclaimed" retirement plan. What is an unclaimed retirement plan you ask? An unclaimed retirement plan is what happens when an employee changes jobs and leaves their vested retirement benefits at the previous employer and through relocation or subsequent moves, the retirement plan from the previous employer now has no way to contact the beneficial owner. In other words, it is a plan left at a previous employer and through combination of mail being returned as undeliverable, phone number changed or disconnected, and previous email account no longer being active, the account is determined to be "unclaimed". Since the average person changes jobs around 11.7 times during their working career; or about every four years, keeping up with balances and monitoring plans and allocations can be a daunting task [1].

Leaving an employer can be a difficult experience in itself, but in this lesson, both husband and wife had several different employer plans that were now "unclaimed" with previous employers. When the couple, Abby and Carter, began calling to see where accounts were and to request forms to consolidate accounts they ran into a few issues. One issue in the search was that the retirement funds were now held through a completely different custodian and took a bit of legwork to find the new custodians contact information. Furthermore, what made this even more challenging was that most of the information on file to authenticate the account had become outdated: incorrect address, closed email, disconnected phone and beneficiaries that were significantly different from the current wishes of the Abby and Carter.

THE ISSUES

- The risk of Escheatment
- Benefiting the wrong or only some beneficiaries
- Investment allocations no longer matching desires of investors

THE LESSONS LEARNED

One of the first issues with unclaimed employer or other retirement plans is the risk of escheatment. What is escheatment you ask? Escheatment is when property is turned over to the state for safekeeping. Considering the average person moves an average of 11.7 times in their lifetime, it's easy for things to slip through the cracks [2]. This can easily occur when important contact information is never updated, such as a new mailing address and/or phone numbers on old retirement accounts. When enough time has passed (usually between three and five years), and a plan is unable to reach the account owner, the process of escheatment begins. Three of the especially painful aspects about this include: the securities inside the account being liquidated, 10% federal tax automatically withheld from amounts paid to the state, and lastly, the custodian is required to report the escheated amount to the IRS as a taxable distribution from the IRA to the owner of the IRA. This distribution creates a 1099-R, even though the amount in the IRA was paid to the state and not the IRA owner [3].

The second issue with failing to take action on old employer plans can be forgetting to update beneficiaries on all of the separate accounts. There are several factors that go into making an informed decision whether to leave the funds with the old employer, transfer to the new employer plan, or to an IRA, such as available fund options, plan fees, and so on. Whichever decision is made, as time goes on and life events happen, beneficiaries may change due to marriage, divorce, the birth of children, adoption, etc. Let's face it, life can get busy and remembering to update one, two, three or more previous employer plans with new beneficiaries can easily get pushed down the priority list. Be proactive! I have seen a number of times that a previous spouse or stepchildren from a previous marriage were beneficiaries. While some states may have some protections from a previous spouse not listed on a divorce decree, it is best to be aware and make sure beneficiaries align with one's wishes.

The third issue with an unclaimed retirement plan is an inadvertent increase in risk allocation. It is not uncommon to have more aggressive or volatile investment allocations early in one's working career. As time goes by, one may forget to review and update investment selections and the person's overall portfolio may actually be significantly more aggressive (or riskier) than a person's comfort level. In periods of market decline, account value may take a substantial fall. Now, to be fair, I have also seen the complete opposite. For example, with a local university, I have seen several cases where the client's money, unbeknownst to them, was sitting in a money market for *years* earning a low rate of interest. This can be just as detrimental to one's retirement, as money not invested and working is money losing purchasing power to inflation (the general increase of the price of items) and missing out on opportunities of compound interest and potential growth.

LESSON #6

POOR SURVIVOR

THE STORY

Don had worked at a local auto manufacturer for decades and was fortunate to be vested in a company pension. When the time came to retire he was presented with several options yet opted to take the single life annuity on his pension (although he was married and his spouse was younger than he). Things looked great with assets totaling around $1 million, their monthly income was nearly $8,000 a month ($3,600 single life pension, $3,100 Don's Social Security and $1,300 in Social Security from his wife).

THE ISSUES

- Life expectancy differences
- Benefit continuation (pension and Social Security)
- Legacy
- Control of assets

THE LESSONS LEARNED

The first part of this lesson deals with life expectancy. Don had selected the single-life annuity option when he chose the way in which he would receive his pension. A single-life annuity option is where the income will only continue during that person's life. This option gives the retiree the highest monthly income among other income options; however, it is also the riskiest for a married couple.

RETIREMENT: WHAT COULD GO WRONG?

Some of the risk from selecting this option comes from the fact that the average life expectancy is approximately 78 years old, meaning half of all people die before and the other half after [1]. With a single life annuity, if the person receives one payment and then passes away, the income stops and the company or plan keeps the remaining funds. The opposite is also true. If the person lives until 110 or longer, the annuity continues paying.

In the story above, we can see how this will begin to cause a few issues with regards to survivor income in the event of Don's passing. When Don dies, not only will the pension of $3,600 be gone, but his wife will also lose $1,300 in Social Security benefits. The result will be the reduction of monthly income amounting to $4,900 / month ($58,800 / year) or an 84% drop in monthly income. *A consultation with a trusted financial advisor is strongly recommended before pension decisions are made!*

After Don chose the single life annuity option, there was little that could be done regarding that decision but there are still several steps that can be taken to help mitigate the risk of an early demise on the annuitant. One possible option would be that the couple takes out a life insurance policy on Don so that in the event of death, a lump sum would be paid to help replenish the lost annuity income. Should Don's wife precede him in death, he can cancel the policy and keep the higher income or opt to keep and leave tax-free legacy to heirs or other organizations.

Something important that I breezed over a moment ago was in regard to the Social Security survivor benefit. One question I receive frequently is, "What happens to Social Security benefits when either the husband or wife die before the other?" Generally, the surviving spouse receives the higher of the two benefits and loses the other. In this case, it certainly helps that the wife gets to step into the bigger Social Security benefit, however, the loss of her $1,300 in addition to the $3,600 pension will really begin to stress the remaining portfolio.

The third and fourth parts involve the leaving of a legacy and the control of investments. Instead of beginning the pension, a person may be able to take a lump-sum payment from the plan and roll the payment into an IRA. It is important to note that not all plans allow a lump-sum payment. Several factors can impact the actual account value, such as the current interest rate environment and life expectancy. The lump-sum option can be a great option if a client wants to have more control over the actual investments, wants flexibility with payments, or desires to have the ability to pass any remaining account value down to future generations.

LESSON #7

INVEST ME NOT

THE STORY

Alyssa was approaching retirement, divorced, and recently unemployed due to employer downsizing. Had it not been for receiving an inheritance of nearly $200,000 from a recently deceased relative, the situation would have been even worse. While Alyssa had been married for nearly a decade, there was little to show besides a mortgage on her house (with several years to go before the mortgage was paid off), a balance on an equity line of credit, and around $10,000 in an IRA (individual retirement account). To cover her living expenses, Alyssa was drawing down on the inheritance at a rate of $1,300 per month. With her earliest ability to draw from Social Security still five years away, the remaining funds really needed to be put to work fast or at least better utilized.

THE ISSUES

- Idle money and inflation
- Debt into retirement
- Social Security benefits for divorcees who were married over ten years

THE LESSONS LEARNED

This story is especially painful on three different fronts. The first lesson is that having too much money sitting idle can be very damaging to a retirement plan. When funds are sitting in a bank account, they are in all probability earning only a fraction of a percent in interest if that. While there is minimal risk to principal with having money in a bank account, there is also minimal reward. The hidden risk in retirement is inflation.

Inflation can be best described as a general rise in the price of goods and services that reduces purchasing power (amount of goods or services that can be bought for a given amount of money). Several examples of inflation of goods would be through the rise in the price of gasoline, milk, bread, houses, etc. There is a saying that grandparents used to be able to go to the movies and get a bag of popcorn for $1.00, not so much the case today.

As mentioned in an earlier chapter, there are significant advantages of using the bucket approach for retirement income planning. Having too much money allocated to the safe bucket means inflation is making the few (albeit safer) dollars able to purchase less and less over time. If a person is willing to take on more risk, in the form of stocks, bonds, or mutual funds, and so forth, then there is a potential for more reward. This reward would be realized through capital appreciation, dividends, etc.

The second lesson from this story is about having debt when approaching and/or in retirement. While we would like to imagine that everyone gets to pick when they retire, the reality is that approximately 37% of people retire earlier than expected due to health, family or even employment issues [1]. Unexpected early retirement can lead to reduced benefits due to early filing of Social Security or pensions (if employed by one of the few companies that still offers a pension). Early retirement can also leave one with a smaller nest egg than initially anticipated. Having monthly payments on top of living expenses can really have a negative effect on the overall success of a retirement plan.

To show the significance of this, I give you an illustration involving an individual who had about $50,000 sitting in her savings account. Currently, this individual had a car payment of $433 per month with a payoff amount of $25,000. I compare two plans side by side, with both plans based on an income of $2,000 per month. The first plan is based on retaining the car payment each month of $433 while letting $50,000 sit in her savings account. The second plan is based on the car loan of $25,000 being paid off with savings account funds and retaining the other $25,000 in savings. The results were glaringly different. The individual's assets lasted nearly twelve years longer had the debt of $25,000 been paid off immediately because of the immediate reduction in the amount of monthly funds needed to cover monthly expenses. Not bad, considering the difference was solely due to cash flow planning and involved no market risk or additional savings.

The third and last lesson in this story is the not-so-well-known issue of Social Security benefits after a divorce. Current legislation allows a person who is divorced and who had a marriage that lasted 10 years or longer to receive benefits based on the ex-spouse's record (even if the ex-spouse remarried). This is true as long as a few criteria are met, such as: unmarried status, age 62 or older, ex-spouse is entitled to Social Security or disability, and benefits you are entitled to on your own record are less than the benefit you would receive based on your ex-spouse's work [2]. Unfortunately, in this scenario, Alyssa's divorce was finalized just *days* before the 10-year mark, sadly making this not an option. Having a financial professional who specializes in retirement income or having a competent attorney involved in financial decisions may help you to make educated choices when retirement planning.

LESSON #8

WORK UNTIL WE DIE

THE STORY

Next we will discuss a couple in their early 60's, Gayle and Harold. What initially was a question about life insurance turned out to be a retirement disaster waiting to happen! While both were currently working full time, the wife had just filed for Social Security benefits. The house was beautiful and, while talking with them, it didn't take long to determine they were house-rich and cash-poor. By this I mean they had spent more of their funds on the equity of their house rather than in accumulating liquid assets for their retirement years. To top things off, the couple had debt which included a leased vehicle in the garage, a loan on their second vehicle, and still had nearly a decade left of future house payments.

THE ISSUES
- Lack of savings and planning
- Debt into retirement
- Insufficient life insurance

THE LESSONS LEARNED

The first lesson in this story is best summed up by Zig Ziglar who would say, "If you aim at nothing you will hit it every time". This is where having a financial advisor who specializes in retirement income planning can really have a tremendous impact on the quality of retirement years.

In this case, with basically no comprehensive retirement plan in effect; the bulk of their income over the years had been spent on having and maintaining a beautiful home. While it's not bad to have a nice home, this spending model left a rather small portion for the accumulation of liquid assets. Their meager amount of liquid assets in retirement accounts would not be able to sustain their standard of living during their retirement years. By both husband and wife continuing to work and the wife recently claiming Social Security benefits, she had given up her opportunity to defer her Social Security benefits, which would have enabled her benefits to grow. In addition, Gayle's taxable portion of income may now increase (depending on the income level). If the sole income was Social Security, there may have been little to no tax at all due to the unique taxation of Social Security. Both the larger Social Security benefits and income from a larger retirement fund account would have been helpful in sustaining a better quality of life in later years.

The second lesson in this story deals with a topic that I feel is truly paramount to a successful retirement - being debt-free. While having a current large annual income can cover up current budget problems, ultimately, debt makes the borrower a slave to the lender (Proverbs 22). The issue stems from the fact that by having debt and making payments, interest is actively working against the borrower. Having debt is literally like going to bed and inviting robbers to rob you while you sleep because, when you wake up each morning, you actually have less money than when you went to bed. The effect of living in debt during retirement is magnified because the assets that are intended to provide income for living expenses, legacy, and so on have to now work even harder. The funds must now cover not only living expenses, etc., but also cover the principal portion of the debt payments and the interest associated with having the debt.

The third issue, and original topic of discussion, was having insufficient life insurance. Someone once told me that life insurance can help solve two very different problems: an estate size problem (estate is too small) or an estate tax problem (estate too large). For this couple, the issue was an estate size problem. In this case, not nearly enough assets had been saved to provide for income in their retirement years or to provide for a surviving spouse, in the case of a premature death. As we can see in their present situation, there is not enough time to save for retirement and even downsizing to a smaller, less extravagant home would only net a limited amount of funds. One of the most efficient ways to make up for lack of funds and shift the risk of a catastrophe, such as a premature death of either the husband or the wife, is by purchasing life insurance to take care of either surviving spouse.

LESSON #9

PLANNING FOR THE UNEXPECTED

THE STORY

Lets call them Mr. & Mrs. Wells. A married and middle aged couple that had been through some serious adversity in life. Mrs. Wells had been in a very serious automobile accident that left her physically and slightly mentally impaired. This serious event not only lead to a shortening of her working career but also required aids to help her with physical therapy and additional required services which Mr. Wells was simply not able or qualified to perform. Mr. Wells had been employed by a very large local Fortune 100 company for several years and had done well financially, acquiring nearly $1 million in company stock in his 401K and a very considerable monthly pension check.

However, as things gradually changed at the company, the local plant was shut down and Mr. Wells was laid off. With several years left to go until Social Security and Medicare benefits took effect, Mr. Wells opted to rejoin the workforce on a full-time basis to help cover the cost of his wife's health aids and to continue to save for retirement. Unfortunately, after several years, it became apparent the health of Mrs. Wells was continuing to decline and she required full-time skilled nursing care, necessitating her transition into a nursing home. Had proper estate planning been in place as soon as the accident occurred, options could have been available to minimize taxes and protect the financial assets of Mr. Wells.

THE ISSUES
- Need for estate planning
- Net unrealized appreciation
- Lack of diversification

THE LESSONS LEARNED

Each of the following lessons is particularly painful because of the number of years the couple could have been planning to prevent a Medicaid spend-down in the event of a prolonged period in a nursing home. As Mrs. Wells was already requiring aid above and beyond what her husband could provide and her condition was not improving, some proper estate planning could have drastically improved the husband's financial outlook.

The first lesson has to do with the need of estate planning for people who are approaching retirement and is paramount when retired. This plan could include the preparation of basic documents such as Wills, Durable Power of Attorney, Durable Healthcare Power of Attorney, etc. In some circumstances a Trust may be beneficial. One of the reasons these documents need to be prepared prior to an event is because in the blink of an eye, a person could become incapacitated or lose the capacity to make decisions. If these documents are not prepared before an event occurs, a person or family may then need to petition the court to establish a conservatorship or guardianship, which can be a lengthy and burdensome process.

To build upon the need for estate planning would be to prepare for long-term care, if the need should arise. The reality is that most people over the age of 65 will need some form of care at some point in their life. This risk can be mitigated in several different ways including but not limited to traditional long-term care, life insurance with LTC riders, annuities, trust, etc.

The second lesson has to do with a tax benefit called the NUA, or Net Unrealized Appreciation. NUA is the difference in value between the average cost basis of shares of employer stock (what it was bought at) and the current market value of the shares. What is important to remember is that while the $1 million in his employer 401k was all in company stock (which had yet to be taxed), the cost basis of the employer stock was only $180,000. Normally, distributions would be considered all taxable income but if this tax benefit had been implemented, Mr. & Mrs. Wells could have paid ordinary earned income tax on the $180,000 and the remaining shares could have received preferential capital gains tax on distributions. This tax could be as low as 0% depending on other amounts of taxable income. Remember, for strategies like this, it is crucial to consider consulting with both financial advisor and a tax professional as there is little forgiveness and several steps required from the IRS on handling this correctly.

The third lesson is on diversification. Instead of the proverbial "having all yours eggs in one basket," having different investments may allow for others to do better over the same period of time as a poorly performing investment. It is important to note that diversification does not ensure gains of prevent the possibility of a loss. Fortunately for Mr. & Mrs. Wells, the company stock that they had been invested in had done exceptionally well. This is not always the case; Enron, Kodak and Blockbuster are examples, to name a few. Something as simple as a big headline in the news or change in the market perception of the company and life savings can be lost in a hurry.

One way that people can help limit large swings in a portfolio is to diversify. For example, imagine a single elevator with one cable holding it up. The one cable represents the stock of one company; for example: Apple. Should something happen to that one cable the elevator can come crashing down. Alternatively, imagine an elevator with multiple cables similar to a mutual fund (i.e. 50-200 several different stocks and or bonds). In the event that one or more cables snap, the elevator may feel the snapping event, but the other cables can help limit a drastic drop and buoy the portfolio.

LESSON #10

OH, MY TAX

THE STORY

A few years ago, I met a single man, never married, who we will call Jason. Jason had done well financially and had acquired close to $800,000 in an IRA. For the past several decades he had rented an apartment and had just recently filed for Social Security, after attaining his full retirement age. With both parents recently deceased, Jason and his five siblings had received an inheritance of the family farm, which amounted to approximately 200 acres with a farmhouse. While four of the siblings wanted to keep their share of the inheritance of acreage and house intact, one of the siblings had been dealing with financial issues related to care for a special needs child. Jason had funds available and had contemplated taking a distribution close to $200,000 from his IRA to buy that sibling's inheritance share. After consulting with a financial advisor, he put a halt to that idea quickly.

THE ISSUES

- Social Security Taxation
- Medicare Part B and D and IRMA (Income Related Medicare Adjustment)
- Tax diversification

THE LESSONS LEARNED

This lesson relates to what implications could have occurred had Jason withdrawn the $200,000 from the IRA. One of the unique aspects of Social Security is how it is presently taxed. Currently, Jason has an income of around $26,000, which is coming solely from Social Security (this income more than covers his $2,000 / monthly living expenses). However, in the eyes of the IRS, the formula to determine what income (in retirement) causes Social Security benefits to be taxable is (adjusted gross income + nontaxable interest + half of Social Security benefit) [1]. In this case, the IRS considers Jason's income as $13,000. Because $13,000 is less than the $25,000 MAGI threshold for someone filing his or her return as an "Individual" for 2019, none ($0) of his Social Security will be included as taxable income [1]. If Jason had pulled out the $200,000 in one tax year, not only would he have had a huge tax bill because the full distribution would have been considered income, 85% of his Social Security benefit would have also been included in his taxable income.

The second issue in this story is the ramification that could have happened to Medicare Part B and Part D premiums, if Jason had taken a distribution of $200,000 from his IRA in one tax year. This issue is one that does happen occasionally and is usually due to a lack of planning and consulting with an accountant and/or financial advisor. This issue can also come up when a sudden, unforeseen event occurs which will have a financial impact, such as the death of a spouse or the sale of a business. When income exceeds certain thresholds, Medicare may make an adjustment known as Income Related Medicare Adjustment (IRMA). This is meant to make those with higher incomes pay more for their health and prescription coverage.

To show the impact an IRMA can have on an individual, let's look at Jason's situation. For an individual with income below $85,000 per year, he will pay the typical $135.50 for Part B (which is Medical coverage) and his normal Part D plan premium for 2019 [2]. However, if he had taken a distribution of $200,000, then his new *monthly* Part B premium would increase the following year to $433.40 per month (319% increase per month) and his Part D plan premium would be whatever the plan he was on + $70.90 per month for the following year [2]. You can imagine how Jason would have felt being "blindsided" had he not consulted with a financial advisor. This is yet another example of why having an advisor who focuses on retirement income planning can be valuable.

The third issue comes from a lack of tax diversification. On one hand, if a person strongly believes that taxes will be lower or income will be significantly lower in the future, limited diversification may be a good play. Remember, however, that after attaining age 70 ½, pre-tax retirement accounts require a minimum distribution be taken and taxed each year. Keep in mind, taxes in general, will likely have very little direction to move but up with rising deficits and expanding entitlement programs. Also, in cases where most of the individuals or couples assets are tied up in pre-tax accounts, large distributions (such as the one Jason almost made) can cause a cascade of effects on other areas of the retirement plan (i.e. Social Security taxation, Medicare premiums, tax brackets, etc.). An item that may have helped Jason would be to have had money diversified outside of the retirement account, such as a taxable retail account (where taxes are paid yearly) or a Roth IRA (where taxes are paid on contributions but then grow tax free and distributions can be tax free). There are pros and cons of each type of account and great topics for discussion with your financial professional.

LESSON #11

THAT WAS A CLOSE ONE

THE STORY

This lesson begins with Tony, who had been building and projecting out retirement for a number of years. Tony had been working at a large automotive manufacturer for nearly three decades and with a pension, 401K and an exceptional retirement package, including things such as: health reimbursement account, retiree health insurance, and stipend for self and spouse when transitioning to Medicare. Tony was counting down the days till he would pull the trigger and exit the factory life once and for all. However, there were a few circumstances outside of his control that significantly impacted the decision and timing of that retirement.

THE ISSUES

- Pension Options: Lump vs. Payments
- Interest rate effect on lump-sum
- Pension plan recalculation date

THE LESSONS LEARNED

The first part of this lesson comes from the different ways that pension benefits can be paid. Typically, pension plans pay benefits in monthly installments and can be set up in several different ways. Options can include "Single or Straight Life" which is usually the highest monthly payment because it is based solely on that individual's life expectancy. However, this option can come at great risk especially for married couples with the possibility of only receiving a handful of payments in the event of a premature death. *Does this sound familiar to Don in Lesson #6?* Another option can include payments that are "Period Certain" or guaranteed to make a certain amount of payments over a period even if the annuitant (person whose life the payment is based on) is deceased.

With a traditional pension, when the annuitant or the annuitant and their spouse (if spousal continuation was elected) pass away, the payments may stop (depending if Period Certain was elected). Another way that some pension plans pay benefits is with the option of a "Lump-Sum" payment. Unlike the monthly payments, having a lump-sum distribution from the plan can allow for more control of how assets are invested, income is produced, and ultimately distributed upon death. This can be a valuable option for those with other sources of guaranteed income or for those that would like to leave an inheritance to spouse, children or other causes important to them.

The second part of this lesson has to do with the impact of interest rates on the lump-sum value of a pension. For a visual, let's imagine a string with two buckets tied on each end; one representing the value of a lump-sum payment and the other interest rates. If you hang the string over a clothesline and raise the interest rate bucket, you will notice that the lump sum bucket goes down. The opposite is also true in that when interest rates are going down, the lump sum bucket will go up (i.e. a bigger lump sum payment). What is the rationale behind this? The lump sum payment is a calculation of interest rates over different periods of time and attempts to put a present value on future payments. Why is this important? The *specific date* each year that the employer's plan recalculates lump-sum values based on rising or falling rates can vary, so being aware of this caveat or working with a financial professional to help you can make a significant difference. For example, if Tony decided to wait one extra day, the recalculation date to the new segmented interest rates, the lump-sum value would have decreased a bit over $50,000. This would have been equivalent to working nearly an entire year. To clarify, this decision was the difference between retiring now and keeping the $50,000 from the higher lump sum versus losing the $50,000 from the lump sum and working an entire extra year to make up the difference.

LESSON #12

FINANCIAL CONUNDRUM

THE STORY

This lesson begins with Rachel. Rachel had a number of questions about how to best address a financial dilemma she was facing: how to take care of aging parents and how early retirement may look if she stops teaching to care for them.

To elaborate, Rachel was an only child and her aging parents were both facing deteriorating health, with dementia and a few other health concerns. Not a surprise, Rachel felt compelled to help her parents, as they had expressed that neither of them ever wanted to be in a nursing home. However, with Rachel living nearly two hours away from her parents, commuting daily or even somewhat frequently throughout the week was exhausting while also working a full-time job as a teacher. In addition, as Rachel was also a divorced mother with a minor child, so it's difficult to even somewhat comprehend the level of stress Rachel was under.

THE ISSUES

- Pension eligibility requirements
- Social Security benefits
- Employment Risk
- Health insurance
- Parental health concerns

THE LESSONS LEARNED

As Rachel had been contemplating early retirement, the first issue I will address involves understanding different requirements that plans can have regarding qualifying for pension benefits: attained age and service requirements. As we can see from a brochure right off of the State Teachers Retirement System (STRS) there are two benefits, unreduced benefit or an early retirement benefit, and the criteria needed to meet each [1]. Unfortunately, for Rachel, the requirements indicated that she would not qualify at this time as she was currently 50 years old and only had 25 service credits.

The second issue is that Rachel will not qualify for Social Security benefits based on her own employment as her entire working career has been working in the public sector as a teacher, where Social Security tax is not paid. This means that pension benefits from STRS would truly be a crucial element if she were to have an even remotely successful retirement. Now, a piece that could benefit Rachel's retirement future is that her previous marriage, prior to divorce, lasted in excess of 10 years; meaning Rachel can receive Social Security benefits based on the record of her ex-husband. Unfortunately, it could still be well over a decade until she could start receiving those benefits.

The third issue I will address relates back to the issue of STRS service requirements. While it may work perfectly that Rachel could step away for a number of years and return to the workforce to get the last few service requirements, as cited in Lesson #7, approximately 37% of all people retire earlier than expected due to factors outside of their control, including employment issues. With requirements such as continuing education, or a possible saturated job market of younger and ultimately cheaper employees, Rachel may be willing and eager, yet unable to return to the classroom at the time she wishes to return.

The fourth issue is one that can wreak havoc on a retirement plan and ultimately deters a significant number of people away from early retirement: health insurance. For Rachel, this entire issue gets even more complex with having to consider health insurance for not just herself, but also for her minor child. If Rachel stops working, she may be able to keep the coverage she currently has through COBRA. COBRA is a health insurance program that can allow the employee and dependents to maintain health insurance for a limited number of months following the loss of job or upon reduction in working hours. However, the cost that Rachel would pay would be the full-unsubsidized cost plus a small percentage as a service charge. There are alternatives and I would highly recommend consulting with a professional who specializes in health insurance.

The fifth and final issue is regarding the declining health of Rachel's folks, and really brings to the forefront that we are dealing with "personal finance". The "finance" side is relatively easy to quantify based off: numbers, facts, historical trends. The "personal" side of coping with both parents declining health and wanting to help and respect their wishes to remain at home is difficult, at best. There may be a few concerns that could help provide clarity, such as safety or level of care required.

In the case of dementia or other cognitive or even physical impairments, is it even safe for the person to be in the house unsupervised? What about their ability to leave the house and not know where they are? Furthermore, is more care required than can be provided within an in-home setting?

In moving forward, Rachel would need to contemplate if she was physically and financially able to fulfill her parent's wishes, while keeping in mind the responsibilities she has to her minor child. An idea could be for the parents to sell their home, downsize, and move closer to Rachel to cut down on her lengthy commute. With the sale of the parents' home, proceeds could fund needed in-home care for as long as possible. This may allow Rachel to stay employed and fulfill her service requirements for STRS while maintaining health insurance coverage for herself and child.

CONCLUSION

As one can now see, there are plenty of things that could go wrong before, during and even after retirement. I hope that the twelve lessons presented have been educational and have given clarity to some of the common and not-so-common pitfalls of retirement. It is my desire that these lessons will facilitate dialogue and provides talking points with your financial advisor, tax professional and estate planner.

NOTES

Lesson #5

1. https://www.thebalancecareers.com/how-often-do-people—change-jobs-2060467
2. https://www.steinwaymovers.com/news/how-many-times-does-the-average-person-move-in-a-lifetime
3. https://www.blankrome.com/publications/irs-delivers-double-whammy-owners-escheated-iras

Lesson #6

1. https://www.cnn.com/2017/12/21/health/us-life-expectancy-study/index.html

Lesson #7

1. https://www.fool.com/retirement/2019/05/06/why-do-so-many-people-end-up-retiring-earlier-than.aspx
2. https://www.ssa.gov/planners/retire/divspouse.html

Lesson #10

1. https://www.ssa.gov/planners/taxes.html
2. https://www.ehealthinsurance.com/medicare/part-d-all/what-are-medicare-part-d-irmaa-and-part-b-irmaa

Lesson #12

1. https://www.strsoh.org/_pdfs/brochures/15-126-pg33-59.pdf

ACKNOWLEDGMENTS

I thank all who helped and inspired me to write this book.

I especially want to thank my wife, Jaime, for supporting me throughout this long and tedious process.

Jordan Settlage, thank you for the push I needed to finally make it happen. Jordan, you are an inspiration and your forward thinking and problem solving will change the world.

Ashley Bell and Lauren Smetzer for helping me edit.

Last, but certainly not least, my mother. Who inspired and motivated me throughout every step of the journey.

ABOUT THE AUTHOR

Rob Neff, RICP® is a financial advisor who specializes in retirement planning and has helped numerous individuals, families, and business owners navigate retirement. He graduated from Bluffton University with a Bachelor of Arts in Business Administration.